Abram, Abram, where are we going?

Fredrick and Patricia McKissack
Illustrated by Joe Boddy

THIS I LOVE TO READ BOOK . . .

- has been carefully written to be fun and interesting for the young reader.
- repeats words over and over again to help the child read easily and to build the child's vocabulary.
- uses the lyrical rhythm and simple style that appeals to children.
- is told in the easy vocabulary of the validated word lists for grades one, two, and three from the *Ginn Word Book for Teachers: A Basic Lexicon.*
- is written to a mid-second-grade reading level on the Fry Readability Test.

To Etheldra Hollis

Chariot Books is an imprint of David C. Cook Publishing Co.
David C. Cook Publishing Co., Elgin, Illinois 60120
ABRAM, ABRAM, WHERE ARE WE GOING?
© 1984 by Fredrick and Patricia McKissack for the text and Joe Boddy for the illustrations
Printed in the United States of America
89 88 87 86 85 84 5 4 3 2 1

Library of Congress Cataloging in Publication Data
McKissack, Fredrick.
  Abram, Abram, where are we going?
  (I love to read)
  Summary: Recounts the Biblical stories about Abraham and how he became the "father of many nations."
  1. Abraham (Biblical patriarch)—Juvenile literature.
  2. Patriarchs (Bible)—Biography—Juvenile literature.
  3. Bible. O.T.—Biography. [1. Abraham (Biblical patriarch) 2. Bible stories—O.T.] I. McKissack, Pat, 1944-   . II. Boddy, Joe, ill. III. Bible. O.T.
Genesis. English. Selections. 1984. IV. Title.
V. Series.
BS580.A3M36   1984   222'.110924 [B]   83-21041
ISBN 0-89191-811-6 (pbk.)
ISBN 0-89191-842-6 (hc.)

Contents

Abram, Abram,

where are we going?

Long ago,
and far away,
at a time
after the beginning,
after Adam and Eve,
after Noah and the Flood,
there lived a man named Abram.

He lived in his father's house.
He lived with his wife, Sarai,
and his brothers
and his nephew, Lot.

One day,

God said to Abram,

"Leave this land and your father's

house.

Go to a place that I will show you.

I will make you the father of many

nations.

And I will bless you."

6

Abram obeyed.

He left his father's house
with his beautiful wife, Sarai.
He left his father's house
with his nephew Lot.
He left his father's house
with his own servants and many
animals.

"Abram, Abram,
where are we going?"
his family asked him.
"Where are we going
when we leave this place?"

Abram answered,

"God will lead us."

And he did.

Abram went to Bethel.

He put up his tent.

He put up the tents of his servants.

Lot set up his tents, too.

Before long, hard times came to the
land.

The family had no food.

The animals had no water.

Abram told his family they had to
move.

8

"Abram, Abram,

where are we going?"

they asked him.

"Where are we going

when we leave this place?"

Abram answered,

"God will lead us."

And he did.

Abram went to Egypt.

He put up his tent.

He put up the tents of his servants

Lot set up his tents, too.

10

Abram said to Sarai,

"The king of Egypt will kill me

so he can marry you.

Tell him you are my sister."

Sarai did as Abram asked.

Still the king took Sarai to live in his

house.

God was angry.

He sent sickness to Pharaoh and his

house.

"Take Sarai and go!" Pharaoh said.

Abram told his family they had to move.

"Abram, Abram,
where are we going?"
they asked him.
"Where are we going
when we leave this place?"

Abram answered,
"God will lead us."
And he did.
He led Abram back to Bethel.
Abram had a new home.
He built an altar to God.

14

"Thank you," he said.

"Thank you for leading me to this

place." (Genesis 12)

Chatter, chatter, bang, boom!

Abram was a very rich man.

He had many cattle.

He had many donkeys and camels.

He had many servants and much gold.

Lot was a very rich man.

He had many cattle.

He had many donkeys and camels.

He had many servants and much gold.

But Lot's donkeys got mixed up
with Abram's cattle.
Nee-moo, nee-moo, nee-moo.
And Abram's donkeys got mixed up
with Lot's cattle.
Moo-nee, moo-nee, moo-nee.

Lot's servants couldn't
get along with Abram's servants.
Chatter, chatter, bang, boom!
And Abram's servants couldn't
get along with Lot's servants.
Chatter, chatter, bang, boom!
Something had to be done.
18

No one was happy.

"We are brothers," said Abram.

"We should not fight.

Our servants should not fight.

Let us part."

He pointed to the huge land lying

before them.

"If you go to the left,"
said Abram.
"I'll go to the right.
But if you go the right,
I'll go to the left."

Lot looked all around.

Which way should I go?

he thought.

The valley was full of green trees and plants.

There was water for his flocks.

"I will go there," Lot said.

"That will be a good place to live."

Lot had chosen the valley.

Abram's family shouted, "Abram, Abram, where are we going?

Where are we going

when we leave this place?"

Abram answered,

"God will lead us."

And he did.

Abram moved to another part

of Canaan.

And God said,

"Look to the north and the south,

to the east and the west.

All the land that you see

I will give to you and your people."

Abram had finally found a home.

A home for himself and Sarai and his

servants.

24

A home for their children and their children's children.

(Genesis 13)

25

A baby named laughter

Many, many, many years later,
God called to Abram.
"Remember my promise to make you
the father of many nations.
I will keep my promise.
Just promise to obey me—
forever and ever and ever."

And Abram did.

So God gave Abram a new name:

ABRAHAM.

It means "Father of Many Nations."

And God gave Sarai a new name:

SARAH.

It means "Mother of Kings."

Abraham laughed to himself.

Ha! Ha! Ha!

But how can I be the father of many nations?

I am 99 years old.

Ha! Ha! Ha!

How can Sarah be the mother of kings?

28

Sarah is 90 years old.

Soon he remembered his son Ishmael.

But he was the son of Sarah's servant.

God knew Abraham's thoughts.
"Sarah will be the mother of kings,
not her servant.
Sarah will have a son.
You will name him Isaac."

A while later Abraham was sitting by
his tent door.
He saw three men coming up the road.

Abraham ran to see the men.
He knew they must be thirsty.
"Let me give you water to drink,"
he said.

Abraham ran to his tent.

"Bring some water,"

he ordered his servants.

"Make some bread quickly,"

he said to Sarah.

When the men had eaten,

one of them asked, "Where is your

wife?"

Abraham answered,

"She is there in the tent."

"When I come back next year,

your wife will have a son,"

said one of the men.

Sarah heard the man's words.

Ha! Ha! Ha! she thought.

How can I have a son?

I am 90 years old.

Ha! Ha! Ha!

How can Abraham have a son?

He is 99 years old.

Ha! Ha! Ha!

The man (who was really God)
knew what Sarah was thinking.
He said, "Why did Sarah laugh?
God can do anything."

And he did.

The very next year Sarah had a son!

She and Abraham named him Isaac.

It means laughter.

Sarah laughed for joy!

"Ha! Ha! Ha!

I am the mother of a son.

Ha! Ha! Ha!

I am the mother of kings.

Ha! Ha! Ha!

Abraham will be the father of many
nations.

God has kept his promise.

He can do anything!"

(Genesis 17, 18, and 21)

The test

Abraham and Sarah loved Isaac very
much.

But they had not believed God when
he had told them they could have a
son.

So God decided to test Abraham.

He wanted to see if Abraham
trusted him.

He wanted to see if Abraham
loved him.

He wanted to see if Abraham
would obey him.

"Abraham, Abraham," God called.

"Do as I say.

Take Isaac to a place I will show you.

Give him to me as an offering."

Abraham's heart was sick.

He loved Isaac very much.

But Abraham loved God even more.

He wanted to obey God.

He wanted to trust God.

Early the next morning,

Abraham put wood on his donkey.

He and his son Isaac

and two servants

walked slowly to the mountains.

"Father, Father, where are we
going?"
Isaac asked. "Where are we going
when we leave this place?"

Abraham answered, "God will lead
us. He always has."
And God did.

For three days they walked to the
mountains.
Slowly . . . slowly . . .
very, very slowly.

Finally, Isaac said,

"Father, we have the fire.

We have the wood.

But where is the lamb for the

sacrifice?"

"God will provide it," Abraham
answered.

He climbed higher and higher
and higher up the mountains.
Isaac walked behind him,
higher and higher and higher.
At last Abraham stopped.
He built an altar.
Slowly . . . slowly . . .
very, very slowly.
Then he laid Isaac on top of the altar.

Isaac was the sacrifice!

Abraham took one last look at his son.

He raised the knife.

"Stop!" called an angel.

"Now God knows you trust him.

Now God knows you will obey him.

Now God knows you love him."

Suddenly Abraham saw an animal
caught in a bush.
He and Isaac gave it to God
as their sacrifice.

Abraham was very happy.
He loved Isaac very much.

He told Isaac to trust God.

He told Isaac to obey God.

He told Isaac to love God.

And God loved Abraham and Isaac

just as much. (Genesis 22)

The good servant's

promise

Abraham lived to be a very,
very, very old man.
But his son, Isaac, did not have
a wife.
He remembered God's promise:
"You will be the father
of many nations."
So Abraham called his servant
to him.
"Find a wife for my son.
Find a wife from my people, far, far
away in the land of Haran."

"But Abraham, Abraham,
how will I know who she is?"
the good servant asked.
"How will I know who she is
in that land far, far away?"

Abraham answered,
"God will tell you."
And he did.

Soon the good servant left.
He took fine gifts for the
new wife.

He took ten of his master's best camels.

Evening came.

Morning came.

Many, many times.

Klump, bump, klump, bump,

klump, bump walked the camels.

Day after day the good servant

traveled to the east.

At last the servant came to the land

where Abraham's family lived.

He stopped near the town well.

"Down, down," he said to the camels.

It was evening.

The women came to the well

to fill their water jars.

The good servant prayed to God.

I will ask one of these young girls

to give me a drink of water.

If she gives my camels water, too,

I will know you have chosen her for

Isaac.

Before he finished praying,

the good servant saw a beautiful,

young girl.

He watched her walk down to the

spring and back again.
Finally he said to her,
"Please give me a little
water from your jar."

Nee-haw, nee-haw said the camels.

They looked hot.

"I will give your camels some water,"

said the girl.

She went back and forth,

back and forth,

back and forth to the well.

Ten camels drink a lot of water!

"Who are you?" the good servant
asked.

"I am Rebekah," she answered.

"Who is your father?"
the servant asked.

Rebekah told him the name
of her father and grandfather.

The servant had found Abraham's
family!

That night the good servant told his
story to Rebekah's father.
He agreed. "It is God's will
for Rebekah to be the wife of Isaac."
So Rebekah and the servant began
the long, long trip back to Canaan.

Evening came.
Morning came.
Many, many times.
Klump, bump, klump, bump,
klump, bump walked the camels.
Day after day the good servant
and Rebekah traveled to the west.

60

One evening they came to a valley.
Some sheep rested near a stream.
Rebekah saw a man running toward
them. "Who is that man?" she asked.
"Isaac," the good servant replied,
"your future husband."

Rebekah was happy.
She loved Isaac.
Isaac was happy.
He loved Rebekah.
Abraham was happy.
Isaac had a wife.
Soon he would have a son.

And God kept his promise to Abraham.
Many people today are the children of
Abraham.
Abraham is the father of many,
many, many nations.   (Genesis 24)